Special Activities and Devotions for Eac

GOD
MADE YOU
SENSE-
ational

BY

DEBORAH SAATHOFF
JANE JARRELL

BROADMAN
&HOLMAN
PUBLISHERS

Introduction to Teaching the Five Senses

God made a world full of beautiful colors, golden sunlight, and sparkling stars. He made cool breezes, soft kittens, and gooey mud. He made birds that sing and people who laugh. His world has smells that can make us happy or warn us of danger.

We find out all about this wonderful world we live in through our senses. God gave people five senses: seeing, hearing, touching, smelling, and tasting. They work to tell your body all you need to know about the world around you. Your senses help keep you safe and help you enjoy the world God made. Wherever you go, whatever you do, all the time, your senses are working.

This book will help you learn more about each of your senses and how you use them. It is written to present complex ideas at an appropriate level for young children. Much of the text can be read aloud to children. Some background information for the teacher is included with each activity along with a list of items you will need to complete that activity.

Each page is organized to include the following:
Teaching Concept
Activity Time
Devotion

As you complete the material, you will find that God truly has made us sense-ational!

SIGHT

A purple balloon floats in a blue sky. A bright pink flower grows above the green grass. A white kitten rolls in the brown dust beside a red barn. These sights may be so common to you that you may not pay much attention to them. But each of these sights is actually part of a miracle: the miracle of sight.

Our eyes may be small but they are a gift from God with a big job to do. You depend on vision more than any other sense to help you find out about the world each day.

Activity Time

What do you see?

Materials needed:
- A live animal such as a dog, cat, rabbit, guinea pig, hamster or gerbil (or a mechanical animal)
- A large sheet of paper
- Markers

Tell the children, "Your eyes see colors and faces. They tell you how big something is, what parts it has, how far away it is, and if it is moving. Your eyes can also help you guess what something might feel like if you touched it."

Allow the children to watch the animal for a few minutes. Then ask the children to name everything their eyes tell them about the animal. (Your list can include color, kind and number of body parts, how it moves and what it does, and if it has long or short hair, just for starters.)

After discussing the list, talk about the fact that you learned all these things by using your sense of sight.

Devotion

Dear God, Thank you for this beautiful world, full of sights to see. Thank you for red and yellow flowers, for dogs that play, for trees that bloom, for birds that fly. Thank you for giving me eyes to see this beautiful world. Amen.

"God saw everything he had made. And it was very good." **Genesis 1:31.**

PARTS OF THE EYE - PUPIL

NOTE: It would be helpful to have ping pong balls available for the children to handle during this section. You will also need Diagram A from the middle of this book.

Is your eyeball really a ball? Yes, your eye is about the size of a ping pong ball with most of it hidden inside your skull. Here is what your whole eye looks like. (Show Diagram A.)

In the middle of each eye, there is a small black hole covered by clear skin. This part of your eye is called your pupil.

Your pupils are like windows. They let in the light. If it is dark, your pupils get bigger to let in more light. If it is very bright, your pupils get smaller to let less light in.

Activity Time

Materials needed:
- A mirror for each child
- Windows and/or lights

Open Sesame!

Tell the children, "You can watch your pupils at work. Hold a mirror in front of your eyes. Watch how your pupils can get smaller and bigger."

Turn off or dim the lights, close the door, and close any blinds or curtains. Wait and watch for at least a minute or two. Open the blinds and turn on the lights.

Ask the children, "What happens to your pupils? Your pupils can change from dark to bright light very quickly. Your eyes may hurt and you won't be able to see for a moment but your pupils will make the change within two minutes. Your pupils will change from bright light to darkness after about 30 minutes."

Devotion

Dear God, Thank you for protecting me. I am so glad you know how much light my eyes need to let in. Thank you for making my eyes that way. Amen.

"He has also made eyes that see." **Proverbs 20:12.**

PARTS OF THE EYE - IRIS

NOTE: As you tell the children about the iris, show them the iris on Diagram A.

When you look at someone's eyes, you usually first notice their eye color. The iris is the colored ring of muscles around the pupil. The iris controls how much light enters the eye by controlling the size of the pupil. The iris helps to protect your eye by letting small amounts of light in since too much light would hurt your eye. Irises can be different shades of blue, green or brown and the muscles make patterns. Each person's iris is a different pattern from everyone else's.

Activity Time

Find out what eye colors you have in your group with this graphing activity.

Blue,

Green,

or

Brown?

Materials needed:
• Several pictures of eyes in each color
• A large sheet of poster board or butcher paper divided into three sections with a band of blue, green, or brown at the top of each section
• Three glue sticks

Ask the children to identify their own eye color. Have them get in lines according to their eye color with all blue-eyed children in one line, all green-eyed children in one line, and all brown-eyed children in a third line.

Ask the children, "Which line is longest? Which line is shortest?"

Hand each child a picture of an eye that matches that child's eye color. Ask the children to glue their eye pictures in a line under the color that matches their eye color.

When the graph is completed count how many eyes are under each color.

Devotion

Dear God, Thank you for my eyes, for the color that they are. Thank you making each of us special. Amen.

"He made us, and we belong to him." **Psalm 100:3.**

PARTS OF THE EYE - LENS

NOTE: As you tell the children about the lens, show them the lens on Diagram A.

Behind each pupil there is a small round shape called a lens. The light coming in from the pupil shines through the lens. The lens bends the light so that it will fit onto a special screen at the back of your eye. The lens in your eye can get fatter or thinner to make clear pictures of near or faraway things.

Activity Time

A magnifying glass can help illustrate how a lens focuses on things up close or far away.

Materials Needed:
- A magnifying glass (at least one, but one for each child would be ideal)
- A small object

Focus!

Place the object on a table and look at it through the magnifying glass.

Ask the children, "Do you need to move the magnifying glass until the object is in focus (no longer looks fuzzy)? Try to hold the magnifying glass where the object was seen most clearly and move the object closer to you or farther away. Is it still clear? Does moving the magnifying glass make the object clear again? Why couldn't it stay in the same place?

"Your lens works like that by changing shape rather than moving back and forth."

Devotion

Dear God, Thank you for giving me eyes that can see clearly, that work whether I am close or far away. Thank you for seeing me clearly and loving me enough to give me eyes to see. Amen.

"Come and see what God has done. See what wonderful things he has done for his people." **Psalm 66:5.**

PARTS OF THE EYE - RETINA

NOTE: Show the children Diagram A from the middle of this book.

The screen at the back of your eye is called the retina. It covers most of the inside of your eye and is made up of tiny parts. Some of these parts are called rods and cones.

Rods and cones help us see well in daylight and dark. Some of these special parts pick up the picture of what we are looking at in black and white. These parts are called rods because they are shaped like straight rods. Rods don't need much light to work. The parts that see color are called cones because they are shaped like cones. Cones need a lot of light to make them work. That is why things seem to lose their color when it gets dark. You need both rods and cones to see.

Activity Time

Materials needed:
- *Mouse Paint* by Ellen Stoll Walsh (Harcourt Brace Jovanovich)
- Red, yellow, and blue tempera paint in three containers
- 3 additional empty containers
- Paint smocks
- Paint brushes
- Paper

Colors of the Rainbow

Read the story to the children and illustrate the color blending using the paints. If possible, allow the students to blend the paints and paint pictures with their new "rainbow" of colors.

Point out that by adding more red than blue makes a different shade of purple than if equal amounts of each color are used or if more blue than red is mixed together.

Tell the children, " You can see how red, blue, and yellow mix to form other colors much the way your brain mixes the color messages from your cones. Our cones vary the amounts of each one as well."

Devotion

Dear God, Thank you for light and dark, day and night, and for eyes that work so I can enjoy both of them. Amen.

"God called the light "day.' He called the darkness 'night.' There was evening, and there was morning." **Genesis 1:5.**

TWO EYES, ONE PICTURE

We can see quite clearly with one eye, so why do we need two? Our eyes cannot be used to look in different directions at once. They work as a pair. Some animals, like rabbits, have eyes on the sides of their heads. They can see all around and watch out for enemies. Your eyes are in front. You can move them from side to side, but you cannot see all around.

Activity Time

Your brain makes just one picture of what you look at using messages sent by both eyes.

Materials Needed:
- A pen, pencil, or popsicle stick for each child
- A wall clock or other distant object

Two

Pictures

Tell the children, "Hold the pen at arms' length and cover one eye. Line the pen up with the wall clock so you see it in the middle of the clock. Uncover your eye and cover your other eye without moving the pen. Did the pen seem to jump? It seemed to move because each of your eyes sees it a little differently.

"Your brain puts the two pictures together so we can tell how far away something is and what shape it is. If you only had one eye, the world would look flat, as it is in a photograph."

Devotion

Dear God, Thank you for both of my eyes. You have made them work together so well. I hope I can work for You, too. Amen.

"We work together with God." **I Corinthians 3:9.**

FOOLING YOUR BRAIN

*S*ometimes you can fool your brain using a special kind of picture puzzle. The pictures fool your brain because they don't seem to make sense. Pictures that do this are called "optical illusions." They can also help to show you that it is your brain that figures out pictures — not your eyes. When your eyes see things that don't make sense, your brain tries to make sense of them.

Hold your thumb up while looking at a person far away. Your eyes say that he looks smaller than your thumb. Your brain is not fooled. The person only looks small because he is far away. Your brain knows that things far away look smaller than they really are. Sometimes it can be fooled.

Activity Time

Materials needed:
• Copies of optical illusions on the next 2 pages

Give each child a copy of the Cat Optical Illusion.

Ask the children, "Which cat is larger? They are the same size. Because the lines look as though they are going away from you, it makes the top cat look like it is farther away. Since your brain knows that things are smaller when they are farther away, it thinks the top cat must be bigger because you are looking at it compared to something that looks like it is close to you (the bottom cat)."

Give each child a copy of the Flower Optical Illusion.

Ask the children, "Which flower has the biggest circle in the middle? They're really the same size. The one on the left looks bigger because your brain is comparing it to the circles around the middle."

Devotion

Dear God, You are so amazing! What a cool way to make my brain work. Thanks for making my eyes solve the puzzles that they see. Amen.

"He sees from one end of the earth to the other. He views everything in the world." **Job 28:24.**

CAT OPTICAL ILLUSION

Which cat is larger? Neither one! They are the same size! The slanting lines makes it look as if the top cat is farther away.

FLOWER OPTICAL ILLUSION

Look at the circles in the middle of each flower. Which one is larger? Neither one! They are the same size! The circle on the left looks bigger because we compare it with the circles around it.

A BLIND SPOT

NOTE: Show the children Diagram A from the middle of this book.

One part of your retina has no rods or cones. This is where all the special tiny threads called nerves come together to make one big nerve called the "optic nerve." Because this area doesn't have any rods or cones, it can't see anything. This place is called the blind spot.

You do not notice the blind spot very often. Your eye moves so often that this small spot doesn't stay fixed on the same place very long.

Activity Time

Materials needed:
• Copies of the Cross Illustration found on the next page

Give each a Cross Diagram. Tell the children, "Look at the two crosses. To find the blind spot in your right eye, hold the crosses at arm's length. Close your left eye and slowly move the crosses toward you. When the cross on the right disappears, you have found your blind spot.

Repeat, using the right eye, looking at the left cross.

Devotion

Dear God, I am so glad You don't have a blind spot when You look at me. You know everything about me, but You still love me. Thank You for loving me. Amen.

"What is love? It is not that we loved God. It is that he loved us and sent his Son to give his life to pay for our sins."
I John 4:10.

CROSS DIAGRAM

There is a small area in every eye called the blind spot, which cannot see anything. When both eyes are open, each fills in the other's blind spot.

To find the blind spot in your right eye, hold the crosses at arm's length. Close your left eye, focus on the left cross, and slowly move the crosses toward you. When the cross on the right disappears, you have found your blind spot.

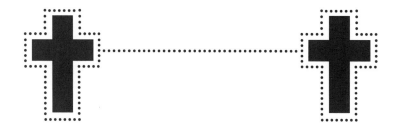

KEEPING YOUR EYES SAFE

You probably already know that it's easier to take good care of something than to fix it after it is damaged. That's especially true with your eyes. God made us so that our bodies help protect our eyes. Tears help to take care of your eyes. If you get something in your eye, tears help wash it out. Eyebrows stop rain and sweat from running into your eyes. Your eyelashes work as traps, stopping bits of dust and dirt in the air from falling into your eye. The bones in your head and your eyelids also help keep your eyes safe.

Activity Time

Safely Tucked Away

Materials needed:
• A book for each child

Tell the children, "Your eyes are safely tucked away inside the bones of your head. Your eyes fit into holes in your skull. Close your eyes. Press a book gently against one side of your face. The book cannot press on your eyes because the bones in your face protect them."

Materials needed:
• Each child paired with a partner

Tell the children, "Your eyelids work as shutters, closing down to let your eyes rest. They also blink very quickly if anything dangerous suddenly comes to close. Your eyes are protected by a special action you can't control that closes your eyelids when anything comes close to them."

Facing his partner, the child should suddenly wave his hands close to his partner's face without touching his partner. The partner will blink every time, even when trying not to.

Tell the children, "This action is called a reflex and it's another way your body helps protect your eyes."

Surprise!

Devotion

Dear God, Thanks for thinking about every little thing like eyelids and bones to protect my eyes. And thank you for taking care of ME. I love you. Amen.

"Turn all your worries over to him. He cares about you."
I Peter 5:7.

WHEN EYES DON'T WORK PROPERLY

The eye has to be perfectly round-shaped to see things clearly. But not everyone has perfectly-shaped eyeballs. Some eyeballs are too long from front to back and others are too short.

Peoples whose eyeballs are too long are said to be nearsighted. Nearsighted people can see nearby objects clearly but have trouble seeing far away. Peoples whose eyeballs are too short are farsighted. They have trouble seeing things that are close to them but can see far away things clearly. Contact lenses or glasses can help correct these problems.

Activity Time

Blind Man's Bluff

Materials needed:
• A blindfold

Tell the children, "Our eyes give us information much more quickly and easily than we are able to get that information without them. This game will show you this."

One child is blindfolded and the other children stand close together in a circle. Spin the blindfolded child around three times and then release. The children clap their hands to signal to the blindfolded child where they are. The blindfolded child finds someone and feels that child's face, shoulders, arms, hands, legs and clothing. The blindfolded child tries to relate shape, size and texture of the mystery child's hair and facial features to those of the person he knows. Then the blind person tries to identify the child he chose.

Ask the children, "How much harder was it to tell what person you chose when you couldn't use your eyes? What clues helped you to figure out whom the person was? What did you want to know about the person that your hands couldn't tell you?"

Devotion

Our eyes are very important and we use them to find out many things about the world we live in. But God says that the things that are most important can't be seen with our eyes. God can't be seen with our eyes. We can't see love or kindness or helpfulness or sharing. Even though we can't see them, we know they are real because we know how they make our lives better when we have them. God said He is everywhere and He sees everything. He never sleeps and there isn't anywhere you can go where He isn't already there waiting.

HEARING

Your ears are the part of you that lets you know when someone says "I love you," or when someone is knocking at the door or what your favorite song sounds like. God made our ears to collect the sounds around us all day long. You can hear happy sounds, like your parents' voices or laughter. You can hear warning sounds like fire engines, smoke alarms, or traffic sounds.

Activity Time

Materials needed:
- A tape of several identifiable sounds such as people talking, water pouring from a faucet, traffic noises, rain, phone or bells ringing, or doors closing. (There are several sound effects tapes available if you would rather not make your own.)
- Optional: Find or make matching pictures to glue on a large sheet of poster board if you think the visual reminders are needed. Just be sure you don't arrange them in a way that corresponds to the order of sounds on the tape.

Sound

I.D.

Tell the children, "You have learned to identify many sounds through your sense of hearing. Your brain remembers the sounds you have heard and helps you to know what a sound is by remembering where you have heard it before."

Play the tape and ask the children to identify (or match) the sounds that they hear. If desired, use the chart you have made to provide a visual reinforcement.

Devotion

Dear God, Thank you for ears that hear. How wonderful it is to hear birds singing, dogs barking, my mom's voice, or beautiful music. You are so good to give us ears. Amen.

"He has made ears that hear." **Proverbs 20:12.**

EAR TO BRAIN!

Your ears send all kinds of sounds to your brain and it tells you which ones to listen to. You are usually too busy to listen to all the sounds your ears hear.

We learn to listen selectively to the sounds around us. Even when we think things are quiet, we can be surprised at how many sounds we hear but don't think about.

Activity Time

Materials needed:
- Paper or chalk/marker board
- Pencil or chalk/markers

How Quiet Is It?

Ask the children to sit as still as they can and not to make any noises. As soon as everyone is still, ask them if the room was quiet. Most will say yes. Then ask them to sit very still again and this time close their eyes and listen very carefully to see if they can hear anything. You should do the experiment with them to help point out sounds later. Allow them to go as long as they are able to, then ask what sounds they heard. Mention traffic sounds, any radio or TV noises from other rooms, voices from people nearby, the hum of an air conditioner or furnace, clocks ticking, rustling from clothes or shoes as children shift in their seats, weather sounds such as wind or rain, someone coughing or sniffling; you get the idea. Count the number of noises on your list. See how much your ears can hear!

Devotion

Dear God, Thank you for the sounds I can hear, even when I am still. I am so glad You can hear me, even when everything is loud. Help me to listen to You. Amen

"Be still, and know that I am God." **Psalm 46:10.**

SOUND

Cod made our ears to hear the sounds around us. Before we can understand just how that happens, it helps to understand more about how sound works. Vibrations produce sound. The following demonstration helps illustrate that idea.

Activity Time

Good Vibrations!

Materials Needed:
- A single-serving size empty yogurt container for each child
- A sharp pencil
- 12 feet of string (kite string works well) for every two children

Make a hole in the bottom of each yogurt container with the sharp pencil. Thread the ends of the string through the holes in the containers from the outside in, making a knot at each end of the string large enough to keep the string from slipping out when pulled taut. Give a "telephone" set to each group of two children. Have the children stand apart with the string between the two containers pulled taut. Each child should take a turn speaking into the container while the other child listens at the other end.

Explain to the children, "Your voice causes the air in the container to vibrate. Those vibrations travel across the tight string to the other container where the other person hears them as sounds.

Devotion

Dear God, It's amazing how every sound is made. Whether it is loud or whether it is soft, a lot happens for a sound to be heard. Help me use the sound of my voice to praise You. Amen.

"Let the sound of the praise you give him be heard." **Psalm 66:8.**

SOUND WAVES

Sound is all around us. Sound waves can travel through water, through the ground, and through windows and walls, as well as through the air. When you hear a sound from outside or from the next room, it has had to go through the air and through a wall, window or door to reach your ears.

Sound waves get weaker as they travel until they just fade away. That's why it's hard to hear things from very far away.

Activity Time

The demonstration described below will help give children a visual picture to use to help understand the concept of "sound waves."

Materials needed:
• A large bowl of water

Making Waves

Let drops of water fall onto the water's surface.

Tell the children, "The ripples that move across the water when the drops fall on it are very much like the ripples sound makes in the air. A noise is like the drop of water. It travels across the air like the ripples in the water. We can't see those noise ripples with our eyes but God made our ears so they can hear them. We call those noise ripples 'sound waves.'"

Devotion

Dear God, Thank you for so many things I cannot see. I can't see sound but I can hear it and know something is there. I can't see You but I know your Spirit is with me. Thank you for always being with me, even though I cannot see you. Amen.

"The wind blows where it wants to. You hear the sound it makes. But you can't tell where it comes from or where it is going. It is the same with everyone who is born through the Spirit." **John 3:8.**

MUFFLED SOUNDS

Soft, squishy things slow sound waves down so that they are hard to hear. If you wear ear muffs or a hood on a heavy coat, the padding slows the sound waves so the sounds get muffled. People who have to work around loud noises at airports or factories often wear special earmuffs to muffle the sounds to protect their ears.

Activity Time

That Alarm's Too Loud!

Materials Needed:
• An alarm clock with a loud alarm
• A thick pillow or cushion

Tell the children, "An alarm clock can help show us how soft things can slow down the sound waves."

Set the alarm to ring. Let it ring for a few seconds then put the thick pillow or cushion over the alarm while it is ringing. Ask the children, "What happened? Why?" If the children do not respond, explain to them, "The soft material in the pillow, slowed down the sound waves so the sound is harder to hear."

Devotion

Dear God, I am so glad you hear me no matter what! You can hear me even when my voice is muffled or even when I just think. Nothing can keep you from hearing me. Thank you. Amen.

"Evening, morning, and noon...he hears my voice." **Psalm 55:17.**

EARS

Our ears are designed by God to pick up the sound waves around us. We can only see the outside part of our ears. The part we can see is called the "outer ear." The rest of our ear, the middle and inner ear, is inside our heads, protected by the hard bones of the skull.

The outer ear, the part we see, funnels the sound waves inside your head through a little tunnel called the "ear canal."

Activity Time

Materials needed:
- A half circle of thin cardboard
- A cardboard toilet paper tube
- Tape

Bring the ends of the half circle's straight edge together to make a funnel. Place the pointed end around the toilet paper tube. Secure with tape.

Tell the children, "Use the funnel to listen to sounds. This is how your ear works. There is a wide opening on the side of your head and a narrow tube inside. The outer ear funnels sounds into the inside, hearing parts of our ears. Some animals, like rabbits, have big outside ears shaped like funnels. Their funnel-shaped ears are able to hear more sounds than our more flat ears can. The funnels we just made helped our ears hear more sounds. That is because the funnel is shaped to catch even more sound waves. We can easily help our ears hear more sounds by making them more like funnels than they already are.

"Listen quietly for a moment. Put your hands behind your ears. Bend your ears forward. Did you hear a difference?"

Devotion

Dear God, I am so glad you made my ears look the way they do and rabbits look the way they do. You knew just what mine needed to be and what rabbits needed to be. I'm glad I can hear sounds and that my ears can "catch" the sounds waves. Amen.

"Those who have ears should listen." **Matthew 13:9.**

HOW YOUR EAR VIBRATES

NOTE: Show the children Diagram B from the middle of this book.

The sound waves that enter your ear go along your ear canal to a very thin piece of skin called your eardrum. When the sound waves hit your eardrum, it makes it vibrate, or move back and forth very quickly. The vibrations move from your eardrum onto three very tiny bones. Then they make a coiled tube deep inside your head vibrate. There's liquid, like water, inside that tube and very tiny hairs. The liquid makes the hairs move. A special nerve in your ear changes the vibrations into messages. It sends the messages to your brain and your brain decides what the sound means.

Both of your ears send messages to your brain. You have two ears because two ears working together can help you know which direction a sound is coming from. The ear closest to the sound will hear it first. Because your brain can tell which ear hears the sound first, you can tell where the sound is.

Activity Time

Materials Needed:
• A blindfold
• Two people
• Two pencils
• Cotton balls

Hide and Seek

Tell the children, "Your ears are very good at telling your brain where a sound is. This game will help show you this."

One child should hide. Have the second child wait (blindfolded) in the center of the room. Tell the hiding child to make a noise or say a word without saying WHERE to look. The child looking can remove the blindfold and look for the hiding child.

Tell the children, "Trying to locate a sound using just one ear is much more difficult. Let's see how that works."

Blindfold one child. The blindfolded child should also wear a cotton ball in one ear. The second child should move around the room tapping the two pencils together. Ask the blindfolded child to point to or face where she thinks the sound is coming from. Now try it again but allow the blindfolded child to use both ears.

Devotion

Dear God, I am so glad that I can just listen sometimes. You have given me two wonderful ears that help me hear. Help me use them to listen to good things. Amen.

"My ears have heard it and understood it." Job 13:1.

BALANCE

Your ears also help you keep your balance. That means you are able to stand up and walk steadily without wobbling or falling over. You may also know how to keep your balance on roller skates or on a bicycle. Your senses of sight and touch help you balance, too, but your ears tell your brain which way is up.

(Show the children Diagram B.) Inside your inner ear, connected to the coiled tube, are three tube-like tunnels with liquid, like water, and very tiny bits like sand inside. When you move your head, the liquid moves too. It pushes against the tiny threadlike nerves that send a message to your brain. These messages tell your brain if your head is up, down, sideways, moving, or still.

Activity Time

Materials needed:
- A clear jar almost full of water
- A spoonful of uncooked rice

Tell the children, "Dizziness is caused by sending the liquid inside those semicircular canals spinning. We can see it happen in the following activity."

Move the jar around quickly so that the water swirls around. Stop spinning the jar.

Ask the children, "What happens to the rice? The same thing happens when you spin around too fast. When you stop spinning, the liquid inside your ears keeps swirling around. Your eyes are telling your brain that you are standing still but your ears are sending messages that you're still spinning. Your brain gets confused and you feel dizzy." (If you have a large, softly surfaced area you might want to let the children experience this sensation by gently spinning them around.)

Devotion

Dear God, Thank you for making my ears this way so I can keep my balance and stand up straight. Thank you for teaching me the right things to do so I can follow you and keep my life straight. Amen.

"In all your ways remember him. Then he will make your paths smooth and straight." **Proverbs 3:6.**

SIGHT

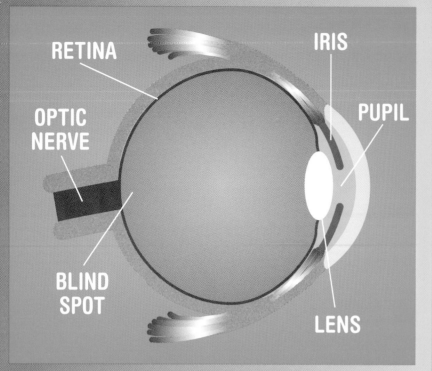

RETINA

IRIS

OPTIC NERVE

PUPIL

BLIND SPOT

LENS

G...
MAD...
SE...
ati...

TASTE

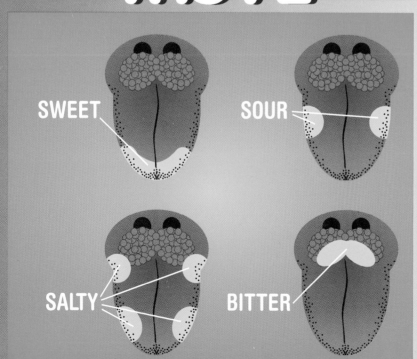

SWEET

SOUR

SALTY

BITTER

HEA...

HAM...

E...

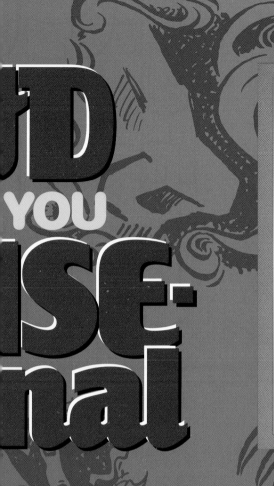

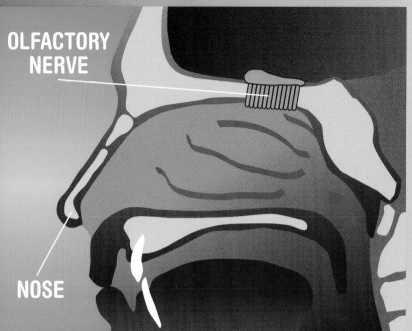

OLFACTORY NERVE

NOSE

RING

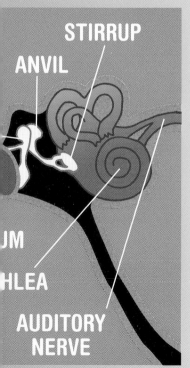

STIRRUP

ANVIL

UM

HLEA

AUDITORY NERVE

TOUCH

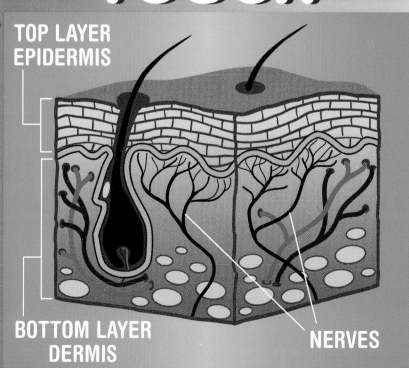

TOP LAYER EPIDERMIS

BOTTOM LAYER DERMIS

NERVES

CARING FOR YOUR HEARING

NOTE: Show the children Diagram A from the middle of this book.

God placed the fragile, hearing parts of your ears inside your head where they would be protected. Your ears can still be hurt, though. Very loud sounds that last too long can cause the delicate inside parts to vibrate more strongly than they are supposed to. When ears have been hurt by too much loud noise, they don't hear high sounds or soft sounds as well. People who work in noisy factories or outside at airports wear special earmuffs to keep their ears safe.

You can also help protect your ears by being careful not to put anything inside them larger than your finger in a washcloth.

Some people cannot hear sounds the way most of us hear them. They are deaf or hearing impaired. Most deaf people hear something but what they hear is either too soft to understand or the sound has been changed and isn't understandable. Their brains work properly but they aren't getting the right messages from the nerves inside their ears.

Deaf people cannot hear what people speak but they can sometimes carefully watch a person's mouth and "read lips" or know what words a person is saying by the way that person's mouth moves. Deaf people can also use their hands to make words. This is called "American Sign Language."

Activity Time

Learning a New Language

Materials needed:
• Chart on the next page showing the American Sign Language alphabet

Practice making each of the letters ahead of time. Help each child spell out his name.

Devotion

God says He always hears us, even if we don't speak our thoughts out loud. He also promises to speak so we can hear Him, but we don't need our ears for that. He has given us His Words in the Bible. He shares His love for us through the Bible, through other people who love Him, and with each one of us through Jesus.

AMERICAN SIGN LANGUAGE CHART

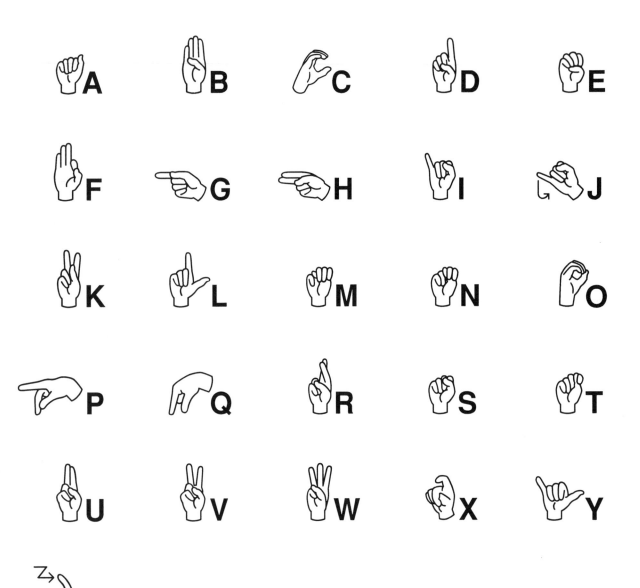

TOUCH

We see with our eyes and hear with our ears but we touch with our skin. Skin covers our bodies and tells us about the things we touch. Our skin tells us when things are touching or pressing on it. Skin can tell if something is hot or cold and it can tell us if something hurts. We learn a lot about the world close to us by touching.

Activity Time

A Touching Field Trip

This activity is designed to help children identify and label many textures that we experience through the sense of touch.
Materials needed:
- A tablet
- A pen
- Large sheets of lightweight paper
- Crayons with the paper removed
- A container of disposable wash cloths (wipes)

Take the materials on a walk with the children. Feel different textures such as tree bark, concrete, bricks, and sand. Let the children make rubbings of the textures by placing the paper over the surface and rubbing the crayon over it using the long side. Label the rubbing. Have them describe the texture (rough, sharp, scratchy, smooth, bumpy) and include that word with the label.

Some feeling words do not lend themselves well to rubbings (sticky, wet) so keep a record of the describing words your child uses in your tablet. Use the wipes as needed.

When you return, talk about the textures and feeling words you experienced. See if your child can add any other words to your list. Post the list where you can refer to it and be sure to display the rubbings.

Variation: You may do this indoors using items such as sandpaper, tile, brick, plaster, or carpet. Provide several additional items in a variety of textures: velvet fabric scraps, netting, wire mesh (screen or strainer), stuffed animals, baskets, mirrors, or pillows.

Devotion

Dear God, I love to touch the smoothness of a blanket, feel the warmth of the sunshine on a hot day, the soft fur of my cat, the cuddly feeling when my mom hugs me. Thank you for giving us the gift of touch. Amen.

"Give thanks to the Lord, because he is good." **Psalm 107:1.**

SEE HOW MUCH YOUR FINGERS KNOW!

Our senses help us learn about our world and we remember much of what they teach us. Our brains remember the information we've received from our sense of touch when we've handled these items before. If we have handled them often, we will identify them more easily. If our brains haven't had this information before, our guesses may not be right.

Activity Time

Touch and Feel

Materials needed:
• Several small familiar items of different shape, thickness and texture (Suggestions: a toothbrush, washcloth, paintbrush, feather, block, toy car or truck, rock, rubber ball, coin, and crayon)
• A box (large enough to easily hold the items and accommodate a child's hand) with a hole cut in the top
• A pair of gloves

Put the items in the box. See if the children can identify the items by touch alone. Try it wearing gloves!

Variations: use shapes (circle, square, triangle, rectangle). School supply stores or catalogs that handle math supplies will carry attribute blocks. These are wooden or plastic blocks in various shapes, colors, sizes and thicknesses. Attribute blocks would work well for this activity.

Devotion

Dear God, I am so glad you know all about me. You can identify me because you know everything about me. Thank you for loving me enough to know me. Amen.

"Lord, you have seen what is in my heart. You know all about me." **Psalm 139:1.**

OUR SKIN PROTECTS US

Our skin also protects us by helping to keep dirt and germs out of our bodies. It keeps the right amount of water inside but doesn't let water from outside our bodies in. Our skin is waterproof! Our skin also stretches when we move and bend.

(Show the children Diagram C from the middle of this book.)

Skin has two layers, a top layer and a bottom layer. We only see the top layer. The inside bottom layer has lots and lots of very tiny threadlike parts called nerves. Nerves are so very tiny we can't see them with our eyes. Nerves find out about what you are touching, or what is touching you, and sends a message to your brain so you know. The nerves work like tiny switches that turn on when they feel a touch, something pressing on you, hot things, cold things or pain (things that hurt). We have more than 20 different kinds of nerves sending 20 different kinds of messages about what we feel.

Activity Time

Materials Needed:
- A bowl filled with warm (but not hot) water
- A bowl filled with room temperature water
- A bowl filled with ice water

Tell the children, "Many nerve endings are sensitive to heat or cold. The following activity shows how our bodies have been made to react to change in temperature rather than just temperature alone.

"Put one hand in the very warm water and another in the ice water. Leave them there for one minute.

"Put the hand that's been in the very warm water in the lukewarm water. It will feel cold because it's not as hot as your skin.

"Now dip the cold hand into the lukewarm water. The water will feel hot!

God made our bodies to work best at a certain temperature. Our bodies work to stay at the temperature God designed for them. We say things are hot or cold compared to the temperature of our bodies. That's why the same water could feel hot and cold."

Devotion

Dear God, Thank you for making me so that my body can take care of me when the temperature changes. No matter how often it changes from hot to cold, you made me so I can change with it. I'm so glad, though, that you don't ever change in your love for me. Amen.

"Give thanks to the Lord, because he is good. His faithful love continues forever." **I Chronicles 16:34.**

TEMPERATURE'S CHANGING!

When you put your hand in hot water, your sense of touch tells your brain that the water is hot and it tries to cool your hand. That's why your hot hand will look redder than the cold one. Your body is sending more blood to your skin.

When you put your hand in cold water, your sense of touch tells your brain that the water is cold and tries to warm your hand. That is why your cold hand will be lighter in color (or even kind of blue) because your body is trying to keep your hand warm. It is making sure your blood gets deeper inside you, away from the very cold temperature.

Your body will also shiver when it's cold to try to get warmer. Your body may also make "goose bumps." Little muscles lift tiny hairs on your skin to try to make a kind of blanket for you. It's a lot like a bird ruffling its feathers when it is cold or frightened.

Sweating is another way your body tries to cool off. It is like pouring water on something hot to cool it off.

Activity Time

Materials needed:
- Small portable fan
- Bowl of water

Tell the children, "Let's see what our sense of touch tells us when we are cooling off. How does your hand feel if you hold it in front of a fan while it is wet?" Dip a child's hand in the bowl of water. Let them hold it close to the fan (supervise carefully, do not let them touch the fan). Observe color change in the hand and let the child describe how it feels. Let each child try this experiment.

Devotion

Dear God, You have given us the neatest things to help us. Whether it is goose bumps or sweat, everything has a reason and a purpose, according to your plan. We are wonderfully made! Amen.

"How you made me is amazing and wonderful. I praise you for that. What you have done is wonderful. I know that very well." **Psalm 139:14.**

YOU HAVE THE NERVE!

Some parts of your body have lots of nerves in them. Other parts don't have as many. The parts that have a lot of nerves are very sensitive, or feel many things very easily. The parts of your body that don't have as many nerves don't feel things as well. They are not very sensitive. The most sensitive parts of our bodies are our lips and fingertips. Each fingertip has thousands of nerves. The bottoms of our feet and our backs are the least sensitive. They don't have as many nerves in them. Our hair and fingernails don't have any nerves in them so we can cut them and not feel anything. We have more pain nerves than any other kind. Pain nerves tell us if something hurts, if it is too hot and burns, or if we have been cut or scraped. We don't like to feel pain but God made these nerves to keep us safe. If you didn't know a stove was hot it could burn you very badly if you left your hands on it.

Activity Time

Materials Needed:
- Old magazines
- Scissors
- Drawing paper
- A red marker
- Crayons
- Construction paper
- Glue

Hands Off!

Trace around each child's hand on a piece of paper. Using a bright red marker, draw a thick circle around the hand and add the diagonal slash meaning "no."

Go through old magazines and cut out pictures of things we do not touch. (Suggestions: knives, fire, space heaters, gasoline, broken glass, electric outlets, certain plants, strange or wild animals). If some pictures you want to include aren't available, you or the children, may draw a picture of it. Glue your pictures onto the construction paper. Glue the "no touching" symbol you made earlier onto the collage.

Talk about the reasons why we don't touch these things.

Devotion

We can close our eyes or wear a blindfold and we won't see. We can cover our ears or wear earplugs and stop hearing. We cannot turn off our sense of touch. Our skin is always sending messages to tell us about the world around us and to help protect us.

Holding a hand when we're scared can make us feel safe. A hug when we're sad can help cheer us up. God uses the people around us to be His hands to touch and comfort us in a way we can feel.

SMELL

ood, smoke, the ocean, gasoline, garbage, animals, perfume, flowers, soap and freshly cut grass are just a few of the everyday odors we smell. Smells are one of the ways you have to find out about your world and experience what God has created for us. The sense of smell helps us to enjoy life and helps us to learn about unsafe conditions. The sense of smell is very important to a person. We say that some things smell good and that some don't. The sense of smell starts with your nose, but it includes other parts of your head and brain.

How does your nose smell? (Show the children Diagram D from the middle of this book.) When a pizza is baking, tiny bits go out of the oven and into the air. These little bits are called molecules. These small pieces of material are too small for us to see, but the nose is sensitive to them as they travel through the air into your nose. When you breathe in air, pizza molecules go into your nose and tickle the nerve endings of the olfactory nerve. (This is a special place high up in your nose where molecules can stick.) Nearby nerves send messages about the pizza molecules to your brain. Then you smell the pizza.

Activity Time

What do you smell?

You can identify many things using your sense of smell.
Materials needed:
• 5 to 10 baby food jars
• Scented items to be placed in each jar (alcohol, flowers, onion, cinnamon, mint, etc.)
• Pictures of each item in the baby food jars (one picture of each item per child)

Each child opens one baby food jar at a time and sniffs. Then the child places a picture of what she thinks is inside on top of the jar. Then children compare results and decide on the correct match after the discussion.

Devotion

Dear God, I love to smell the ocean, fresh bread baking, cookies in the oven, fresh air after a rain, hot pizza, freshly-picked flowers. Thank you for giving me these wonderful smells that remind me of wonderful things. Amen.

"He richly provides us with everything to enjoy."
1 Timothy 6:17.

SMELL IS SENSITIVE

$\mathbf{S}$mell is remarkable because it is extremely sensitive. Some scientists estimate that smell is 10,000 times more sensitive than taste. It responds to extremely small numbers of molecules.

People have a very weak sense of smell compared to animals. Many animals, such as dogs, deer, and bears, can smell much better than people. Bees are attracted to flowers because of their sweet smell. They use smell to find their food. Animals use smell to warn them of danger. A deer can detect the smell of a hunter; a mouse can detect the smell of a cat.

Activity Time

Animal

Noses

Materials needed:
• Pictures or picture books containing photos of animals noses that include a variety of distinct noses such as a pig, dog, rabbit, anteater, tiger, elephant, and horse.

Tell the children, "Animal noses are shaped much differently than ours to help their sense of smell. Animals rely on this sense much more than people do."

Show pictures of the animals. Ask the children, "Whose noses and mouths are these? Some animals hunt others and use smell to hunt. Smell also warns them of danger." Look at all the pictures and name the animal that goes with the nose.

Devotion

Dear God, I love the way you have made all of us different, that all the animals have everything special they need. Thank you for taking care of us. Amen.

"You made me and formed me with your own hands."
Psalm 199:73.

SMELLS GO AWAY FAST

There is another way that your sense of smell is different from all other senses. Smell is the fastest adapting of all our senses. You've noticed this when you come across a strong and unpleasant odor. You smell it for a short time then, after a while, your sense of smell gets tired. When you first come into your home, you can smell dinner cooking, but after a few minutes pass, your smelling nerves get overtired. Then you don't smell anything at all.

Some smells make you feel happy, others sad. Some smells make you feel hungry. Others can make you feel sick. Smells can also remind you of the places and times where you have smelled the smell before, like the smell of roast and potatoes baking in your grandmother's kitchen or the smell of warm cinnamon sugar cookies when you walk in the mall.

Different places have their own smells. Hospitals have a smell. Bakeries have a smell. Can you think of other smells that remind you of certain places?

Activity Time

Materials needed:
• Sandpaper, cut into 2" squares
• Cinnamon sticks
• Scissors
• Yarn, cut into enough 12" lengths for each child to have one
• A hole punch

Remember...

Give each child a piece of sandpaper, half a cinnamon stick, and a length of yarn. Instruct the children to rub the sandpaper with the cinnamon stick. Punch a hole at the top of each square. Put a piece of yarn through the hole to make a necklace. Ask each person to tell what the cinnamon stick makes them think of.

Devotion

Dear God, It is really neat how you even made smells unique. No two smells are alike just like no two people are alike. Thank you for making each of us, and so many things, different. I like being special. Amen.

SMELL MEMORIES

Many smells trigger memories. They can remind us of people we know, places we have gone, or something we have done. God made us this way to help us remember special people and special times.

Activity Time

What Does This Remind You Of ?

Materials needed:
- Coffee
- Popcorn (popped)
- Rose
- Aftershave
- Perfume
- Orange

Place each of these items in a bag that zips close. Let each child smell these things. Ask the children, "Where would you usually smell them? Does it remind you of someone? Does it remind you of something you did?" Let each child share her experiences.

Devotion

Dear God, Smells remind me of so many things. Cinnamon makes me think of fresh baked cookies and how much I love my mom. I can smell bread baking and feel hungry. I smell alcohol and think of my doctor and how he helps me get well. Thank you for all these things you give me. Amen.

"He is the God who made the world. He also made everything in it. He is the Lord of heaven and earth." **Acts 17:24.**

DIFFERENT FACTS ABOUT SMELLS

SMELLS CAN WARN US OF DANGER

Smells can warn you not to eat bad food or tell you that something is burning. Smell helps you to recognize danger: fire, escaping gas, or rotting food. How does the sense of smell warn us of danger? What other ways does the sense of smell help us in times of need?

SMELLING UP CLOSE

The harder you sniff the stronger the smell. Compare smelling something that smells good (a rose) by sniffing very close and by breathing regularly farther away. When you sniff, you pull air straight up your nose. More molecules stick near the nerves so you get more of the smell.

Some people develop their sense of smell for a special use. A perfume maker can tell all the different flowers from each other by their different smells.

Activity Time

Fragrant Art Work

Materials needed:
- Tempera paint
- Essence oils or extracts
- Paper
- Paint brushes
- Drop cloths
- Painting smocks or aprons

Stir the flavorings or oils into the tempera paints. Paint pictures with the various colors that would smell like the object painted. (Violet oil would be stirred into a purple paint, a pine scent would be stirred into green.)

Discuss the color and the smells and where they could be found. Let the children paint.

Devotion

Dear God, You have found so many ways to take care of us. You even use smells to help us keep away from danger. Or to make us feel happy. Or to make us feel loved. Thank you for using all these things to show how much you love us. Amen.

"So we know that God loves us. We depend on it. God is love."
I John 4:16.

SMELLS MOVE!

Your nose is a simple sense organ. Your eyes, your ears, and your skin have many more different parts and different jobs. But your sense of smell is very important to you. Not only does it let you know what smells good and what doesn't, but your sense of smell helps you taste the food that you eat. Actually, a large part of your sense of taste is really your nose sending your brain messages about smell at the same time.

Both nice smells and nasty smells move in the air. Strong smells can spread a long way.

Activity Time

Materials needed:
- A strong scent, such as rubbing alcohol or vinegar
- A piece of cloth

Put a few drops of the scent on the cloth. Have the children close their eyes. Wave the cloth. Ask the children to raise their hands as they smell the smell. Where does the smell move?

Devotion

God gave the flowers their beautiful smells and made our noses so we could enjoy them. He gave our food a smell, too, and our bodies use it to help us taste food while we eat. Smells help us enjoy our world more and that's the way God planned it!

TASTE

Tart and tangy lemonade, sweet and sugary candy, bitter medicines and salty french fries are all a part of our sensational sense of taste. Stop and think of your very favorite food and thank God that we have the ability to taste. Taste helps us, among other things, to choose and enjoy food.

The tongue is the main body part we use for tasting food. We eat with our mouths and taste with our tongues. Our tongue has help from the water or saliva in our mouths. If we did not have the saliva in our mouths, our food would not melt or dissolve and we could not taste it.

Activity Time

If Your Mouth Were Dry

Materials needed:
- M&M's™
- Sweet Tarts™
- Paper towels
- Sugar
- Small plastic spoons
- Glasses of water

Give all the children an M&M™ and instruct them to put it on the top of their tongues and not to bite or suck on it. Ask the children, "Can you taste the candy? No, we have to get it wet with saliva, chew it and mix more saliva with the candy before we can begin to taste it. The saliva mixes with food and spreads all over the tongue; then you can taste the candy. Now suck or chew the M&M™. Can you taste it now?

Dry the top of your tongue. Put a little sugar or a Sweet Tart™ on your dry tongue. Will you be able to taste it? Now take a drink of water. Taste the sugar or Sweet Tart™ again. When the water or saliva is on your tongue, the sugar melts and you taste the sweet taste."

Devotion

Dear God, It is amazing that, with just a little taste, we can tell whether something is good or bad, sweet or sour, salty or bitter. We also need to know just a little bit about you to know how good you are and how much you love us. Thank you for taking care of us. Amen.

"Taste and see that the Lord is good. Blessed are those who go to him for safety." **Psalm 34:8.**

TASTE BUDS

Look at your tongue in the mirror. Can you see lots of little bumps? Inside each bump there are more than one hundred taste buds. The taste buds pick up different tastes in your food. The tongue is a muscle covered with many small bundles called taste buds that have many nerve endings. Nerve endings are little feelers on your tongue that send important clues to your brain.

If you took a big bite of a warm chocolate chip cookie, little tiny bits of that cookie or molecules would go into the bumps or taste buds on your tongue. As soon as those little bits hit the feelers, or nerve endings, a taste message would be sent to your brain. Then you would know what you were tasting.

Our sense of taste can also warn us if a food is not safe to eat. Some things look good, but can be very dangerous. It is never a good idea to taste something that is not familiar to you until you find out what it is.

THE FABULOUS FOUR

Different parts of your tongue have small bundles or taste buds that perform different jobs. We can only taste four different flavors - sour, salty, bitter and sweet.

(Show the children Diagram E from the middle of this book.)

Activity Time

The Tongue Test

Materials needed:
- A piece of red construction paper for each child
- Markers
- Scissors
- Magazines
- Glue

Help each child cut their construction paper into the shape of a tongue. Instruct the children to use a marker to draw the four sections of the tongue where you found the different tastes.

Let the children look through the magazines and cut out pictures that they think will match each different taste and glue them on the area of the tongue where you would taste that flavor.

Devotion

Dear God, You have given us all kinds of flavors to enjoy. I love chocolate, hamburgers, spaghetti, carrot sticks, popcorn, and french fries. They are all different but are all wonderful to eat. Thanks for giving us so many different things to enjoy. Amen.

"He gives food to every creature. His faithful love continues forever." **Psalm 136:25.**

TASTE TEST

Your tongue knows four different tastes: salty, sweet, sour, and bitter. Your tongue has special places to tell each taste that it knows.

(Show the children Diagram E from the middle of this book.)

Activity Time

Where Do You Taste It?

Materials needed:
- 4 cotton swabs for each participant
- Salt
- Sugar
- Lemon juice
- Coffee grounds

Tell the children, "Use cotton balls or cotton swabs to dab bits of salt (salty), sugar (sweet), lemon juice (sour) and coffee grounds (bitter) on your tongue. Can you tell where the different flavors are picked up on your tongue?"

NOTE TO TEACHER: On the next 4 pages are recipes you may duplicate and send home with the child to prepare and taste.

Devotion

Dear God, You even made special places on my tongue! There is a place for everything in your world and everything you have made is good. Thank you for all the wonderful things you have made. Amen.

"Sing to him. Sing praise to him. Tell about all of the wonderful things he has done." **I Chronicles 16:9.**

FUN WITH FLAVORS - BITTER

Bitter: The taste buds which taste bitter things are at the back of your tongue. A bitter flavor is strong and often unpleasant. Can you name some bitter foods?

Here is a recipe for the bitter taste your tongue knows. Try this at home. Ask an adult for help with making this recipe.

Activity Time

BITTER BALLS
1 can frozen orange juice, thawed
1 stick butter, softened
1 large box of vanilla wafers, crushed
1 box powdered sugar
1/2 cup unsweetened cocoa

Utensils needed:
• large mixing bowl
• spoon
• measuring cup
• wax paper

1. Mix the first four ingredients thoroughly.
2. Roll the dough into walnut-sized balls.
3. Roll the balls through the unsweetened cocoa.
4. Refrigerate until thoroughly chilled, about one hour.
   Makes 2 dozen.

Other bitter foods: coffee, olives, tea, banana peel, semi-sweet chocolate

Devotion

"When you are hungry, even what is bitter tastes sweet."
Proverbs 27:7.

FUN WITH FLAVORS - SWEET

Sweet: The taste buds which taste sweet things are tasted at the front of your tongue. That is why you lick a lollipop or an ice cream cone. A sweet flavor contains sugar or has the taste of sugar. Can you name some sweet foods?

Here is a recipes for the sweet taste your tongue knows. Try this at home. Ask an adult for help with making this recipe.

Activity Time

ANIMAL CRACKER SANDWICHES
16 animal crackers
1/2 cup strawberry cream cheese
4 large strawberries, sliced

Utensils needed:
• 1/2 measuring cup
• knife
• cutting board

1. Place 8 animal crackers flat side up on your work surface.
2. Spread the animal cracker with strawberry cream cheese.
3. Top the cream cheese with a slice of strawberry.
4. Place an animal cracker flat side down on the strawberry slice to create your sandwich.
   Serves 8.

Other sweet foods: honey, candy, raisins, milk chocolate

Devotion

"I want you to know that wisdom is sweet to you. If you find it, there is hope for you tomorrow. so your hope will not be cut off." **Proverbs 24:14.**

FUN WITH FLAVORS - SOUR

$\int$our: The taste buds which taste sour things are tasted at the side of your tongue. A sour taste is sharp and acidic like lemon juice or vinegar. Can you name some sour foods?

Here is a recipes for the sour taste your tongue knows. Try this at home. Ask an adult for help with making this recipe.

Activity Time

LITTLE LEMON TARTS
12 mini tart shells
1 jar prepared lemon curd (or lemon pudding)
l fresh lemon
whipped cream (optional)

Utensils needed:
• knife
• cutting board
• spoon

1. Place prepared tart shells on a plate.
2. Spoon lemon curd into the tart shells.
3. Place lemon on a cutting board and slice. Cut slices into fourths or wedges.
4. Place lemon wedges on top of lemon curd.
   Serves 6.

Other sour foods: grapefruit, sour candies, sour cream, plain yogurt, vinegar, dill pickle, lime

Devotion

"Those who look to the Lord have every good thing they need."
Psalm 34:10.

FUN WITH FLAVORS - SALTY

Salty: The taste buds which taste salty things are toward the front of your tongue. Salt is a white substance that is made up of crystals. It is used to flavor and preserve foods.

Here is a recipes for the salty taste your tongue knows. Try this at home. Ask an adult for help with making this recipe.

Activity Time

SALTY POTATO WEDGES
1 (16 ounce) package of frozen potato wedges
1 teaspoon salt
1/2 teaspoon pepper
1/2 teaspoon paprika
1/2 teaspoon garlic
Butter flavored cooking spray

Utensils needed:
• cookie sheet
• measuring spoons
• reclosable plastic bag
• spatula

1. Place frozen potato wedges on a cookie sheet.
2. Spray the cooking spray on a cookie sheet.
3. Put seasonings into a reclosable plastic bag.
4. Add potato wedges to the bag and shake until thoroughly coated.
5. Bake according to directions on potato package.
   Serves 4 to 6.

Other salty foods: nuts, popcorn, cheese, crackers

 ## Devotion

"You are the salt of the earth."   **Matthew 5:14.**

TASTE AND SMELL ARE MIXED UP

The inside of the nose and the mouth are joined. As we eat we smell, so smell helps taste. Smelling is a very important part of tasting.   The taste of food depends on what it smells like as well as what it really taste like.   When you have a cold or your nose is stuffed, can you smell your food? Does your food have a good taste, or does it all taste the same?

Activity Time

Materials needed:
- Two pieces of pear, apple, and potato for each participant
- A knife
- A cutting board

Tell the children, "Close your eyes and hold your nose. Now, taste the pieces of pear, apple and potato you have.

"Try it without holding your nose. Is there a difference?

"If you don't smell the food can you tell the difference between the taste of pear, apple and potato?"

Devotion

Dear God, You have given us so many good things to eat. Then you put our bodies together in such a way that we can really enjoy all these good things. Thank you for these good, good things. Amen.

"Every living thing looks to you for food. You give it to them exactly when they need it. You open your hand and satisfy the needs of every living creature." **Psalm 145:15.**

TASTING TEXTURES

Texture is the look, feel and sound of a food. Crisp and crunchy carrots, crusty and chewy bread, soft and fluffy whipped cream or a thick and creamy milkshake are examples of the many different textures food can come in.

Each tiny food molecule sends different messages to the tastebuds. No one knows exactly how this happens. But somehow our brains understand the different tastes. Your brain also receives other information about the things you eat or drink. These tell your brain if something is hot or cold, thick or thin.

The tongue gives information about how the food feels or its texture. The taste of food also depends on whether it is crisp, soggy, smooth or lumpy. These feelings are felt through touch and pressure nerves on your tongue. Your sense of feeling helps tell you that a potato chip is crisp and crackly and a peanut is small and smooth, that sugar is grainy and syrup is liquid. To really enjoy eating, you need three senses: taste, feeling and smell.

Activity Time

Texture

I.D.

Materials needed:
- Carrot sticks
- Peanuts
- Slices of bread
- Crunchy peanut butter
- Smooth peanut butter
- Caramels

Give each child a taste of each item. Help them identify textures as smooth, crunchy, chewy, lumpy, etc.

Devotion

Dear God, I love the way all these things work together! The nose needs the tongue and the tongue needs the nose. We need everything to make it work. All parts of my body need each other just like I need my parents, my friends, and you to make me work! Amen.

"The body is not made up of just one part. It has many parts. God has placed each part in the body just as he wanted it to be." **1 Corinthians 12:14, 18.**

SUMMING IT ALL UP!

WE ALL WORK TOGETHER

All the senses work together to help you enjoy eating. Other senses (eyes, ears and touch) give more information about what you are eating. Your eyes tell you whether something looks good to eat. Your ears pick up sounds while you are eating —- the crunch of celery or the snap of a cracker. Your brain puts all of this together along with the help of your taste and smell senses to give you the joy of eating.

FOOD MEMORIES

Your brain remembers where and when you taste certain foods. You can be surprised by tastes when they are different from what you are used to. You sometimes expect things to taste different from the way they do. Lemon juice sucked through a peppermint stick creates a surprise for your tastes. You know that a lemon tastes sour and peppermint candy tastes sweet. What do you get when the two flavors are mixed? Taste buds taste sweet and sour — but the brain is confused because it remembers lemon and peppermint as flavors that don't happen together.

Activity Time

Helping your taste buds learn is a fun thing to do. Here are some ideas for fun ways to try new tastes (or enjoy familiar ones).
- Flower tasting party - cauliflower or broccoli
- Leaf tasting - cabbage, mint, spinach, parsley
- Seed tasting - sesame, wheat, rice, peas, sunflower, peanuts, popcorn
- Root tasting - carrots, turnips, rutabagas, leeks

Devotion

God created our bodies to need food to stay healthy and work the way He meant for them to. We have to eat, but God designed our tongues and our noses so that while we eat we can have fun tasting all the wonderful flavors He made.

God made your senses so you could find out all about the wonderful world He has given us. As you use your senses to learn about your world, remember God already knows all about you! He will always be with you as you explore the world around you.

SENSORY FIELD TRIPS

Your senses are the ways you find out about the world God made. Here are some places you can go where you will use some or all of your five senses:

BAKERY
CONSTRUCTION SITE
RESTAURANT
NURSERY
FARMER'S MARKET
HOSPITAL OR NURSING HOME
FISH MARKET
BOTTLING PLANT
LANDFILL
APIARY
BOTANICAL GARDEN
SWIMMING POOL
MOVIE THEATER
ART MUSEUM
NATURE TRAIL
CAMPFIRE
SYMPHONY
SKATING RINK
TRAIN (OR BUS) STATION
MALL
HARBOR
ZOO
AMUSEMENT PARK
AIRPORT
DAIRY OR FARM
SEASHORE
GROCERY STORE
SPORTS STADIUM OR ARENA
BALLPARK
PARK
PLAYGROUND